MW00892518

A Spoonful of Songs

A Collection of songs for young children compiled by
Miss Charlotte

Copyright 2015 Charlotte Thistle.
Made in the USA.

Cover art by Harry Andrew Karcher.

All illustrations by Harry Andrew Karcher

except zebra logo by Thomas Little, "I've Been Working on the Railroad"
from iClipart.com & "Sur le pont d'Avignon" from Clipart of LLC.

~ For Ella ~

Acknowledgements

A small and dedicated group of people helped make this book and CD possible. I especially wish to thank Harry Andrew Karcher for his beautiful artwork and for being so generous with his time and creativity, Conrad Uno, the best co-producer and sound engineer in the world, and the musicians who put their time, energy and creativity into the recordings. Particular thanks goes to both Joel Tepp, who put in dozens of hours in the studio, and Andy Short, who put in dozens of hours of practice. Without the contributions of these fine artists, "A Spoonful of Songs" would not be what it is today. In addition, I wish to thank my mother, who was my greatest benefactor and most loyal friend throughout my life, my lovely daughter Ella, for inspiration, and all the families who have participated in my music classes in the last three years for giving me a reason to put this collection together.

I hope you and your family (or students) have as much fun listening, singing and dancing as we had putting it all together!

Miss Charlotte

Table of Contents

ISBN: 1517309727
ISBN 13: 9781517309725

Preface

In 2012 I began teaching music and movement classes for young children in a dance studio in Seattle, WA. As an educational supplement, I photocopied some sheet music into a booklet and did some very rough home recordings of the songs we were singing in class. The classes were fun and the supplemental materials soon took on a life of their own. Parents approached me regularly to tell me that my CD was their child's favorite thing to listen to and that it was on repeat in their car. Delighted, I took the songs into the studio and invited some talented musical friends to join me. Three years later, I have recorded over a hundred songs for children and put together five song collections of approximately 25 songs each.

For the first time, "A Spoonful of Songs" brings some of these songs out of my classroom and into the greater community. In this booklet you'll find some of the most popular songs from my classes, and on the CD, the best recordings of them we have to offer. If you don't have the CD yet, I strongly encourage you to obtain a copy, as the book and CD are designed to work together.

"A Spoonful of Songs" may be enjoyed at home or used in a classroom setting. I've included notes for teachers and parents to help you lead musical activities, and I refer readers to my YouTube channel, "Miss Charlotte's Music for Tots", which has video demonstrations for some of the songs. I've also included guitar and ukelele chords on the sheet music and supplemental chord charts for reference.

The music in this book is primarily designed for children age six months to five years with a parent, caregiver or teacher. Additionally, children ages 6-8 may enjoy playing some of the easier songs on a ukelele or guitar.

In an effort to make the songs accessible for beginning players, including children, I've suggested using a guitar capo on some songs. If you prefer to play those songs on a guitar without a capo, simply refer to the ukelele chords instead, which will appear on the line above. Ukelele and guitar chord charts are provided in the front of the book.

Ukelele Chords

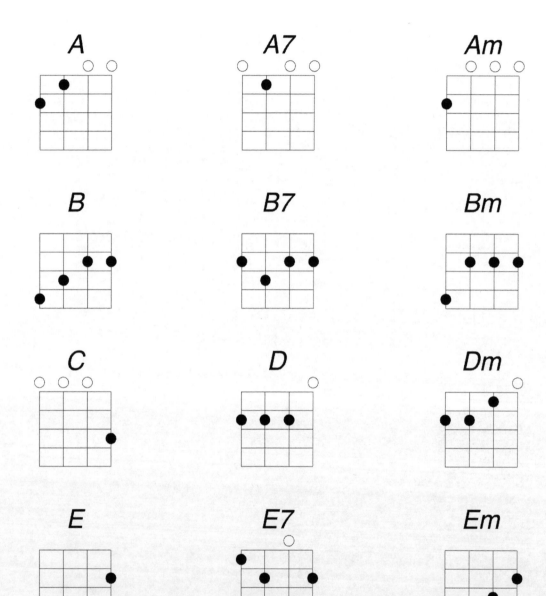

Created using Songsheet Generator.

Ukelele Chords

F
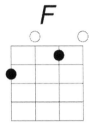

F#
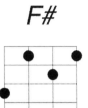

F#7
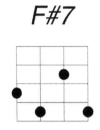

F#m
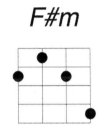

G
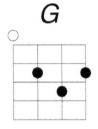

Gm
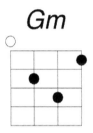

Bb
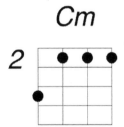

Cm

Created using Songsheet Generator.

Guitar Chords

A
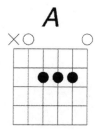

A7
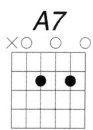

Am
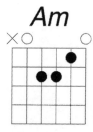

B
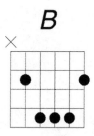

B7
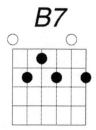

Bm
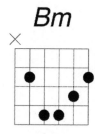

C
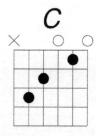

D
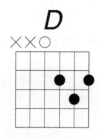

Dm

E
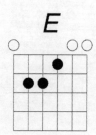

E7
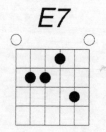

Em
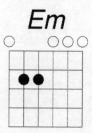

Created using Songsheet Generator.

Guitar Chords

Bb
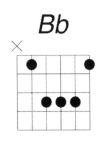

Cm
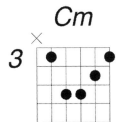

F
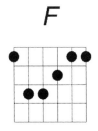

F#
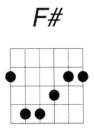

F#7
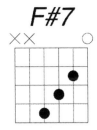

F#m
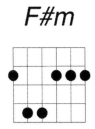

G
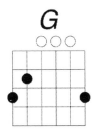

Gm
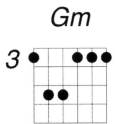

Created using Songsheet Generator.

Dragon On My Knee

Ella Archer

Charlotte Thistle

There's a   ba - by dra-gon on my knee   there's a   ba - by dra-gon on my
ca - ter pil - lar on my   toe   there's a   ca - ter pil - lar on my
cro - co-dile on my tongue   there's a   cro - co-dile on my

knee   well I don't know why he's there but he makes me feel scared. Ma-ma
toe   well I don't know why he's there but he makes me feel scared. Ma-ma
tongue   well I don't know why he's there,but he makes me feel scared. Ma-ma

please get that dra - gon off my   knee!   There's a
please get that cater pillar off my   toe!   There's a
please get that croco-dile off my   tongue!

There's a dinosaur on my nose ...
There's a hippopotamus in my ear ...

One day, in the back of the car, my daughter started playing a game:
"Mama?"
"Yes, sweetie?"
"There's a baby dragon on my knee!"
"Oh! Really?"
"Yes! And you know what else?"
"What?"
"There's a caterpillar on my toe!"

As soon as I got home, I picked up my guitar, and the song, "Dragon On My Knee", was born.

We sing this song in a circle in class. I start off by singing and playing the first two verses. Then I comp on the first chord and ask "Does anyone else have any animals that are giving them trouble today?" Hopefully, a child will volunteer an animal. "And where is that animal?" I ask.

Younger children may need a bit of prompting from a caregiver, but children of ages 3 or 4 will usually get the hang of it and jump in immediately, making up animal-on-their-body scenarios.

Hey Diddle Diddle

Traditional Lyrics

Original Melody by Natasha Marsh
Arranged by Andy Short & Charlotte Thistle

Guitar Chords:

A mom friend of mine, who is also a fabulous jazz singer, made up this original melody for "Hey Diddle Diddle" and was singing it to her son. I asked if I could use it in my class and she said yes!

We play spoons on this one. I have a collection of about 50 teaspoons that I picked up at the Goodwill. I tell each child to take two spoons and show them how to bang the round backs of the spoons together to make a nice clear sound. We also take turns banging on our neighbor's spoons in the circle. For more ideas on what to do with the spoons, please see my Miss Charlotte's Music for Tots YouTube channel.

Ladybird, Ladybird

I set this traditional rhyme to an original melody and made up a fingerplay to go with it. Please see my Miss Charlotte's Music for Tots YouTube channel for a demonstration of the fingerplay.

Traditional Lyrics

Music by Charlotte Thistle

La - dy - bird, la - dy - bird, fly a - way___ home.___ Your

house is on fire and your chil - dren are___ gone. All___ but one,___ his

name is Lit - tle John. He___ is hid - ing be - neath the grind - le stone.

Swingin'

This song has movements that go with it. Please see my <u>Miss Charlotte's Music for Tots</u> YouTube channel for a demonstration.

Charlotte Thistle

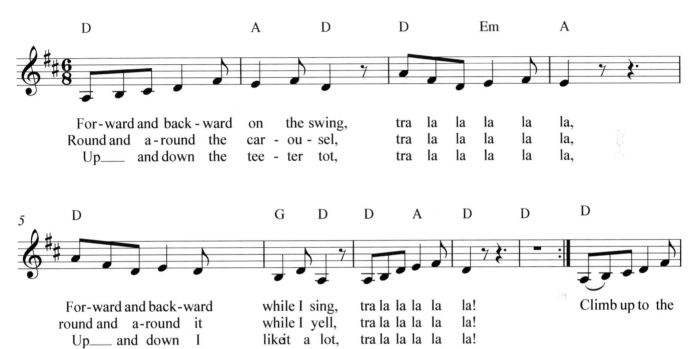

For-ward and back-ward on the swing, tra la la la la la,
Round and a-round the car - ou - sel, tra la la la la la,
Up___ and down the tee - ter tot, tra la la la la la,

For-ward and back-ward while I sing, tra la la la la la!
round and a-round it while I yell, tra la la la la la!
Up___ and down I like it a lot, tra la la la la la!

Climb up to the

A   D   D   Em   A   D

top   of   the slide,   tra la la la   la   la,   Get   to   the top   and

G   D   (NC)

go   for   a   ride,   Whee!_____

The Three Little Pigs Rap

by Charlotte Thistle

When I do this in class, I get all the kids to do the wolf howl with me. I also tap the rhythm patterns out on the floor and have the kids tap them back in a call-and-response.

The other day, I overheard my four-year-old daughter reciting the whole thing to her dollies!

****

This here's a story 'bout three little pigs
who went to build some brand new digs
The first one got a load of hay
and built himself a house that way
The next one built a house of sticks
and the third one built his house with bricks
Everything was goin' strong
Til the Big Bad Wolf came along

(Owooooooooooooo!)

He went on over to the house of hay
that the first little pig had built that day

He went:
(ad lib call and response knocking)

"Little Pig, Little Pig, let me come in!"
"Not by the hair of my chinny chin chin!"
"Then I'll huff and I'll puff and I'll blow your house down!"

(blow)

And he blew that house right to the ground
The little pig went running off like lightnin'
sayin' "My oh my, that was fright'nin'!"
He ran to his brother's house of sticks, sayin'
"Help me brother, I'm in a fix!
That Big Bad Wolf is on my tail

You better let me in and do not fail!"
Well, he got inside just before
That Big Bad Wolf came knockin' at the door

He went:
(ad lib call and response knocking)

"Little Pigs, Little Pigs, let me come in!"
"Not by the hair of our chinny chin chin!"
"Then I'll huff and I'll puff and I'll blow your house down!"

(blow)

He blew that house right to the ground
The little pigs went running off like lightnin'
sayin' "My oh my, that was fright'nin'!"
They ran to their brother's house of bricks, sayin'
"Help us brother, we're in a fix!
That Big Bad Wolf is on our tail
You better let us in, and do not fail!"
Well they got inside just before
That Big Bad Wolf came knockin' at the door

He went:
(ad lib call and response knocking)

"Little Pigs, Little Pigs, let me come in!"
"Not by the hair of our chinny chin chin!"
"Then I'll huff and I'll puff and I'll blow your house down!"

(blow 3x)

But he couldn't blow down the house of bricks
And the three little pigs lived happily ever after.

Rub-A-Dub-Dub

Traditional
Arranged by Charlotte Thistle

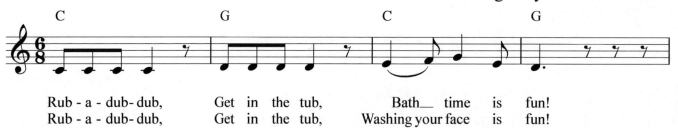

Rub - a - dub- dub,　　Get in the tub,　　Bath__ time is fun!
Rub - a - dub- dub,　　Get in the tub,　　Washing your face is fun!

Rub-bing and scrub-bing and rub-a-dub dub-dubbing and when_____you're clean,you're done!
Rub it and scrub it and rub - a-dub-dub it and　　when it's clean,you'redone!

Rub-a-dub-dub, get in the tub
Washing your hands is fun!
Rub 'em and scrub 'em and rub-a-dub dub 'em
And when they're clean, you're done!

Rub-a-dub-dub, get in the tub
Washing your hair is fun!
Rub it and scrub it and rub-a-dub dub it
And when it's clean, you're done!

In my parent/tot class, we sing "Rub-a-Dub-Dub" in the circle and I
have each little one sit on their caregiver's lap. On the first two lines of
each verse, "Rub-a-dub-dub, get in the tub, washing your hair is fun!"
we bounce them up and down. Then, on the last two lines, "Rub 'em
and scrub 'em and rub-a-dub-dub 'em …", we rub and scrub their hair
as if we were washing it. We repeat this pattern for toes, belly, hands,
face, knees, etc. In between verses, I comp on the guitar, sing "What
else shall we scrub in the tub?" and await suggestions for the next body
part to wash.

Be warned - some funny things can happen. Once, when I asked for
suggestions for what to wash next, a three-year old girl who had
obviously been getting some early anatomy lessons at home, shouted
out "Vagina!" (Needless to say, we didn't act that one out!)

Spin Me Around

Original Lyrics
by Charlotte Thistle

Traditional

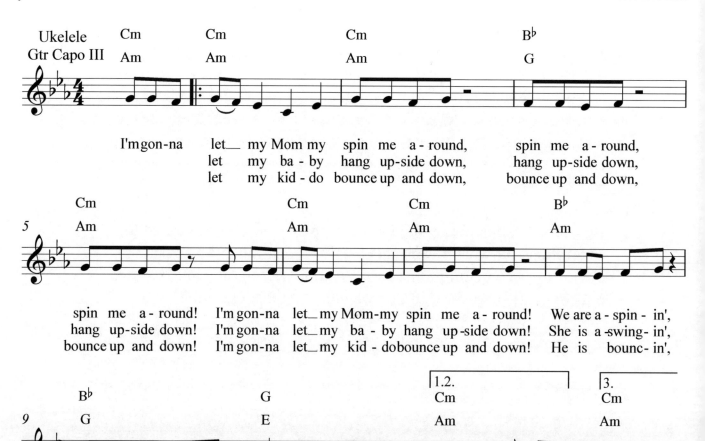

I'm gonna let little Ella fly like a plane,
fly like a plane, fly like a plane
I'm gonna let little Ella fly like a plane
She is flyin', yes she's flyin',
Flyin' like a plane!

I'm gonna let young Henry piggy-back ride!
Piggy-back ride, piggy-back ride!
I'm gonna let young Henry piggy-back ride,
He is ridin', yes he's a-ridin'
Goin' for a piggy-back ride!

"Spin Me Around" is based on a traditional negro spiritual and civil rights marching song which is rumored to have been an underground railroad song before that. The original title is "Don't Let Nobody Turn You Around" and it is speculated that the earliest version of the words is meant to encourage those who planned to escape slavery on their journey to freedom. As a civil rights song, it became "Ain't Gonna Let Nobody Turn Me Around". It's a very powerful song and I encourage you to listen to one of the traditional versions if you haven't already. Sweet Honey in the Rock does a particularly wonderful rendition.

I learned the song when I was a member of the Seattle Peace Chorus and I've sung it in marches myself. As serious as the message of the song is, I chose to have a little fun with it for the kiddos. My intention as a teacher would be to use this version as a bridge to introduce the traditional version of the song, along with a discussion about its meaning, when the kids are older.

The actions are hopefully self-explanatory. But just in case ... on "spin me around", we pick up the little ones and spin them around. The bigger kids can also just spin around on their own. On "hang upside down" we hang them upside down, or they can just bend over and hang upside down all on their own, and so on.

Una Sardina

This is a traditional Mexican children's song and fingerplay. Please see my <u>Miss Charlotte's Music for Tots</u> YouTube channel for a demonstration of the fingerplay.

Author Unknown

Un - a sar - di - na, un - a sar-di - na, na - dan-do en el a - gua, un - a sar - di - na,
Un___ pul-pi - to, un - pul-pi - to, na-dan-do en el a - gua, un___ pul-pi - to,
Un a tun,___ un a- tun,___ na-dan-do en el a - gua, un a tun,___
Un ti-bu ron,___ un ti-bu ron,___ na-dan-do en el a - gua, un ti-bu- ron,___
Un - a ball e - na Un - a ball-e - na, na - dan-do en el a - gua, un - a sar-din - a,

un - a sar - di - na, glu! glu! glu! *(spoken)* Oh no! fue co-mi-do por...
un pul - pi - to,
un a - tun,
un ti - bu- ron,
un - a ball - e - na, (BURP) (Perdoname!)

> English translation:
> una sardina - sardine
> un pulpito - baby octopus
> un atun - tuna
> un tiburon - shark
> una ballena - whale
>
> A sardine, a sardine
> is swimming through the water
> a sardine, a sardine,
> glug, glug, glug!
> Oh no! He got eaten by ...

When the Kids Go Marchin' In

Kids can march, run, jump, dance and mime playing
instruments along with the verses in the song.

Original Lyrics
by Charlotte Thistle

Traditional

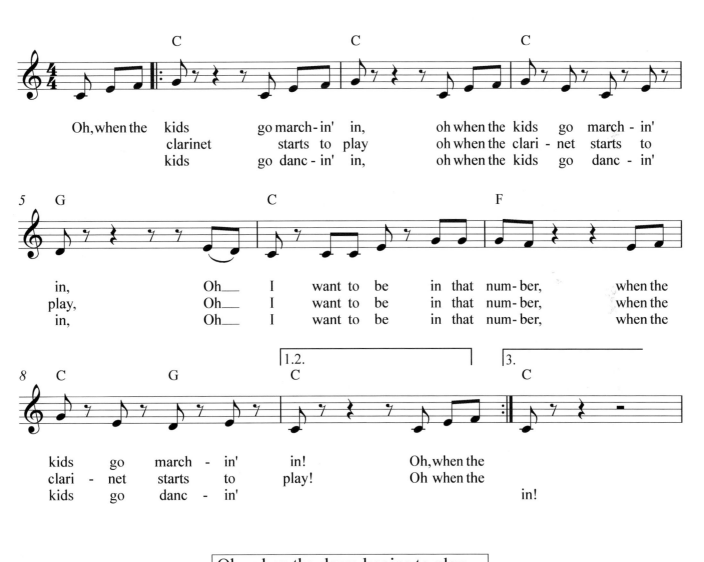

Oh, when the drum begins to play ...

Oh, when the kids go jumping in ...

Oh when the kids go running in ...

Oh when the kids tiptoe around ...

The Itsy Bitsy Spider

I added a few new verses to this classic song. Please see my Miss Charlotte's Music for Tots YouTube channel for a demonstration of the accompanying fingerplay.

Traditional
Arranged by Charlotte Thistle

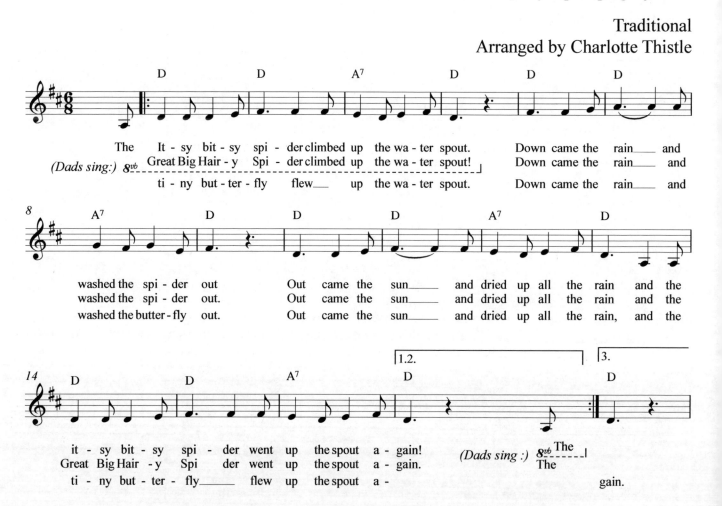

The It-sy bit-sy spi-der climbed up the wa-ter spout. Down came the rain___ and
(Dads sing:) 8vb Great Big Hair-y Spi-der climbed up the wa-ter spout! Down came the rain___ and
ti-ny but-ter-fly flew___ up the wa-ter spout. Down came the rain___ and

washed the spi-der out Out came the sun___ and dried up all the rain and the
washed the spi-der out. Out came the sun___ and dried up all the rain and the
washed the butter-fly out. Out came the sun___ and dried up all the rain, and the

it-sy bit-sy spi-der went up the spout a-gain! (Dads sing :) 8vb The
Great Big Hair-y Spi-der went up the spout a-gain. The
ti-ny but-ter-fly___ flew up the spout a- gain.

The itty bitty frogs jumped up the water spout
Down came the rain and washed the froggies out
Out came the sun and dried up all the rain
And the itty bitty frogs jumped up the spout again

The itty bitty inch worm climbed up the water spout
Down came the rain and washed the inch worm out
Out came the sun and dried up all the rain
And the itty bitty inch worm climbed up the spout again

Frere Jacques

We sing this traditional French song in the circle as a round.

Jean-Philippe Rameau

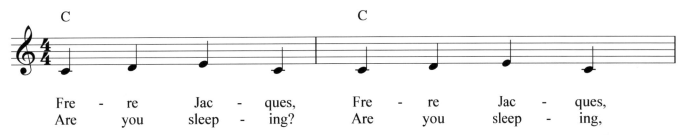

Fre - re   Jac - ques,   Fre - re   Jac - ques,
Are   you   sleep - ing?   Are   you   sleep - ing,

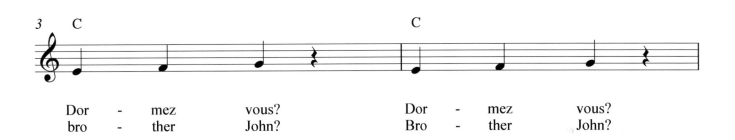

Dor - mez   vous?   Dor - mez   vous?
bro - ther   John?   Bro - ther   John?

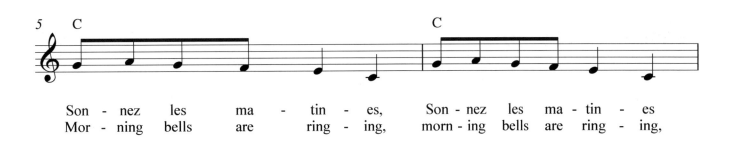

Son - nez   les   ma - tin - es,   Son - nez   les   ma - tin - es
Mor - ning   bells   are   ring - ing,   morn - ing   bells   are   ring - ing,

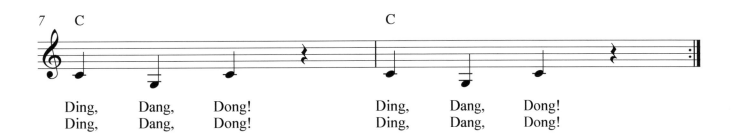

Ding,   Dang,   Dong!   Ding,   Dang,   Dong!
Ding,   Dang,   Dong!   Ding,   Dang,   Dong!

Big Scary Monsters

Original Lyrics by Charlotte Thistle

Traditional folk melody

"Big Scary Monsters" uses the melody of the traditional British sailors' song, "Spanish Ladies". The tune dates back at least to the 1700s and the traditional lyrics tell a sad story of a time when English sailors were ordered to abandon Spanish wives, lovers and children they had become attached to while on overseas assignment, and sail back to England alone. The chorus begins, "We'll rant and we'll roar, like true British sailors …"

When we do "Big Scary Monsters" in class, we dance around and act out some of the movements described in the song, such as rolling eyes, gnashing teeth, waving paws, swinging in the trees, and so on. This is definitely a classroom favorite – the kids really love it!

Looking Through A Hole

Charlotte Thistle

Look-in' through a hole in the fence, what do I see, what do I see? I'm

look-in' through a hole in the fence, what do I see, what do I see? I see a
I see a
I see a
I see

lit - tle boy swing-in' on a great big swing way up in the trees. A
lit - tle girl skip-pin' with a skip-ping rope, jump-ing up and down. A
lit - tle dog dig - gin'__ a great big hole, look-ing for a bone. A
big kids climb-in up____ rung by rung to get to the top of the slide.____

lit - tle boy swing-in on a great big swing, rid - in' in the breeze!
lit - tle girl skip-ping with a skip-ping rope, skip-ping all a - round!
lit - tle dog dig - ging__ a great big hole, so he can take it home!
Big kids climb-ing up_____ rung by rung, and going for a ride! (Whee!)

30

On "Looking Through a Hole", we play with creating a "hole in the fence" by cupping our hands around one eye on the chorus, and acting out the movements (digging a hole, swinging, skipping etc) on the verses.

The Grand Old Duke of York

Original Lyrics by Charlotte Thistle

Traditional

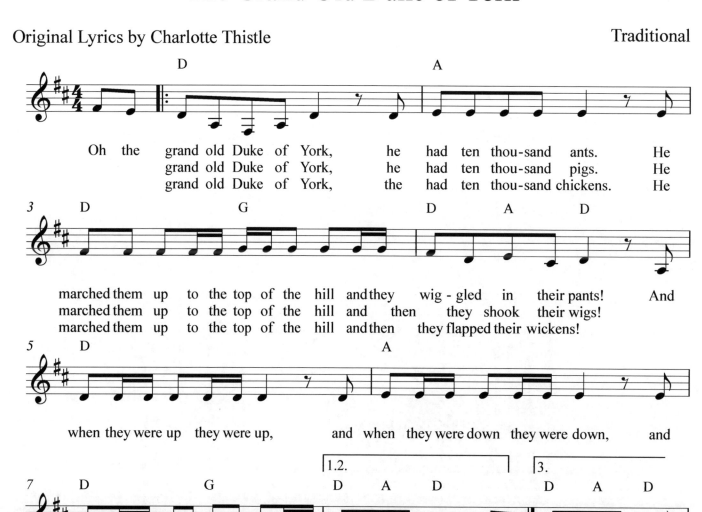

Oh the grand old Duke of York, he had ten thou-sand ants. He
grand old Duke of York, he had ten thou-sand pigs. He
grand old Duke of York, the had ten thou-sand chickens. He

marched them up to the top of the hill and they wig - gled in their pants! And
marched them up to the top of the hill and then they shook their wigs!
marched them up to the top of the hill and then they flapped their wickens!

when they were up they were up, and when they were down they were down, and

when they were on-ly half way up they were nei-ther up nor down. Oh the nei-ther up nor down.

Oh, the grand old Duke of York,
He had ten thousand ducks.
He marched them up to the top of the hill
singing "Qwuk, qwuk, qwuk, qwuk, qwuk!"

Oh the grand old Duke of York,
He had ten thousand feet.
He marched them up to the top of the hill
Stomping to the beat!

Oh the grand old Duke of York,
He had ten thousand bellies.
He marched them up to the top of the hill
And wiggled them like jelly!

Oh, the grand old Duke of York,
He had ten thousand knees.
He marched them up to the top of the hill
And kicked them in the breeze

Oh, the grand old Duke of York,
He had ten thousand bums.
He marched them up to the top of the hill ,
A-Rum pum pum pum pum!

Oh, the grand old Duke of York,
He had ten thousand hands.
He marched them up to the top of the hill
And clapped them with the band

In class, we act out the movements to "The Grand Old Duke of York" starting with marching, then wiggling our pants, shaking our 'wigs', flapping our "wickens"(wings) etc. On the chorus, we reach up to the sky on "up", crouch down on "down" and do a half-squat on "halfway up". And yes, my version of this song is very, very silly! I promise you, though, the kids enjoy it.

****

The original lyrics to "The Bells of London" (on the overleaf) go :

" 'Oranges and Lemons'
say the bells of St. Clements,
'You owe me five farthings',
Say the bells of St. Martin's.
'When will you pay me?'
Say the bells of Old Bailey."

The rhyme continues, mentioning several other churches in London, and ends with the debtor's head being chopped off!

I learned the song as a child, and love the melody, but felt the subject matter and the complexity of the lyrics weren't ideal for kids under five. I replaced the traditional words with the onomatopoeiaic vocables, "ding" and "dong", and added a melody line meant to imitate a familiar peal of church bells.

We sing the ostinato with one or both of the melody lines (depending on the ability level of the class). I have never tried to do the "tick tock" speaking part with the under-five age group and wouldn't recommend doing so, although it could be an interesting poly-rhythmic challenge for older kids.

The Bells of London

(See previous page for notes.)

Traditional Melody
Arranged by Charlotte Thistle

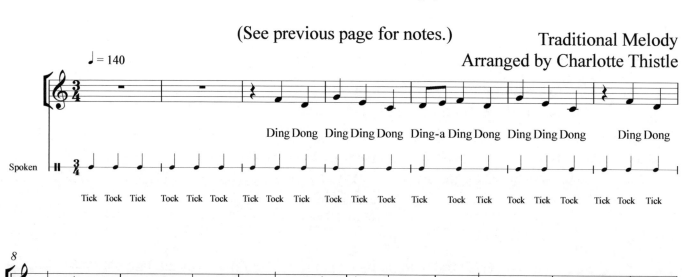

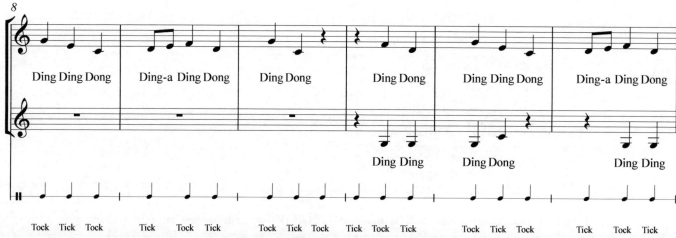

2

The Caterpillar

Adapted from text and melody
by Emilie Poulsson
Arranged by Charlotte Thistle

Fuz-zy lit-tle cat-er-pil-lar craw-ling on the ground   fuz-zy lit-tle cat-er-pil-lar

no-where to be found   when the cat-er-pil-lar's fur-ry coat be-comes too tight, he

spins up a coc-coon   and sleeps there day and night   now we see it mov-ing   his

lit-tle head we spy   now the cat-er-pil-lar   be-comes a but-ter-fly!

The original version of "The Caterpillar" was written and composed by Emilie Poulsson in the 1800s. I took some creative license in editing the lyrics for brevity and modifying the melody to suit.

The little ones really love this fingerplay. Please see my Miss Charlotte's Music for Tots YouTube channel for a demonstration.

Los Elefantes

Traditional

Un e - le -fan -te   se ba-lan-ce-a -ba   so bre__ la te - la de'un a   - ran   -   ya
Dos e - le fan - tes   se ba-lan-ce - a - bran   so bre__ la te - la de'un a - ran   -   ya

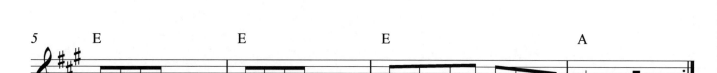

co mo__ve - i - a   que re - sis-ti - a   fue a llam-ar ot-ro e - le - fan   -   te!
co mo__ ve - i - an   que re - sis-ti - a   fue-ron'a llam-ar ot-ro e - le - fan   -   te!

English Translation:

One elephant was swinging
on a spider's web
when he saw that it supported him
he called another elephant to join him

Two elephants were swinging
on a spider's web
when they saw that it supported them
they called another elephant to join them

Los elefantes is a traditional Mexican children's song. When I do it in class, I use a collection of elephant finger puppets and I sing as many verses as I have children in the class (I have thirteen elephant puppets and never more than 12 children per class). For each verse, I pull a puppet out of my waist pouch, put it on my finger, and make it dance around until a child claims it by grabbing it and pulling it off (they learn this game quickly). So, at the end of the song, each child is holding a finger puppet. I then collect the puppets, singing "Adios, elefantes!"

I've Been Working On the Railroad

Traditional

We often use egg shakers with "I've Been Working on the Railroad", and make a train that winds around the classroom and sometimes even out the door and back in again, if our location permits. I encourage the class to pull an imaginary train whistle as we sing the "toot toot"s.

In an effort to keep it simple, I opted to omit "Someone's in the Kitchen with Dinah", which is actually a separate song, historically speaking, although most modern versions present the two songs together as a medley.

Sur le pont d'Avignon

Traditional French

Sur le pont d'A - vig - non, l'on y dan - se, l'on y dan - se,

sur le pont d'A - vig - non, l'on y dan - se tout en ronde.

molto rall.

Les be - bes font comme ca, et puis en - core,_ comme ca!
Les ma - mans font comme ca, et puis en - core, comme ca!
Les jeune filles font comme ca, et puis en - core, comme ca!
Les gar - cons font comme ca, et puis en - core, comme ca!

Translation:	The babies go like this ... (crying)
On the bridge of Avignon,	And again, just like this ...
We are dancing, we are dancing,	The mamas go like this ... (shhh)
On the bridge of Avignon,	The girls go like this ... (curtsy)
We are dancing, round and round.	The boys go like this ... (bow)

"Sur le pont d'Avignon" is a traditional French song and circle dance named after a bridge in Avignon, where the song is supposed to have originated. The song dates back to the 1500s and there are a number of different versions. Older children may do the dance in male-female pairs. However, in my class, we all hold hands and walk around in a circle on the chorus. Then we stop, drop hands and mime the actions that go with the verses.

The traditional verses may include soldiers saluting, abbeys praying, men and women bowing and curtsying and so on. I use verses that are more age and modern culture-appropriate, such as babies crying, mommies shush-ing, girls and boys bowing and curtsying, etc. I also often include animals such as frogs or bunnies jumping, kitties pawing, elephants waving their trunks – really anything I can think of that has a good clear motion or sound effect to go along with it. You could do cars, bicycles, joggers, birds, airplanes. The possibilities are endless.

Sometimes I sing the verses in English so the kids can understand easily, or sometimes I just sing them in French and let the class figure out what the subject is from the movement and/or sound effect that goes with it.

Basque Lullaby

Florence Hoare

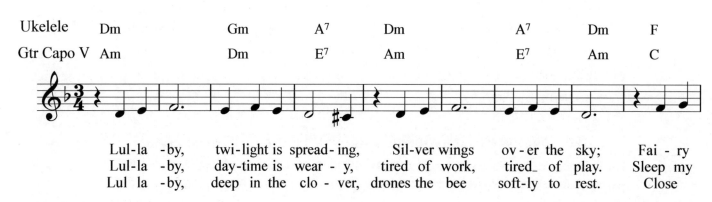

Lul-la -by, twi-light is spread-ing, Sil-ver wings ov-er the sky; Fai - ry
Lul-la -by, day-time is wear - y, tired of work, tired_ of play. Sleep my
Lul la -by, deep in the clo - ver, drones the bee soft-ly to rest. Close

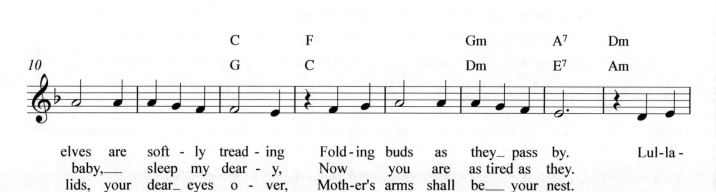

elves are soft - ly tread - ing Fold-ing buds as they_ pass by. Lul-la -
baby,__ sleep my dear - y, Now you are as tired as they.
lids, your dear_ eyes o - ver, Moth-er's arms shall be__ your nest.

by, whis-per and sigh,__ Lul-la - by, lul - la - by.

The lovely "Basque Lullaby" was written by a female composer and lyricist named Florence Hoare. I was unable to find much information about her, but the first known publication of the song was in 1917 so it seems reasonable to assume that she lived around this time.

At lullaby time in class, we sit in a circle. I encourage the kids to lay down or snuggle with their caregiver, and I encourage everyone to sing or hum along to the best of their ability. Often we turn off the lights (it's essential, of course, to have SOME light source, such as a window or a lamp, that remains). I let the older kids take turns with the light switch, one turning the light off at the beginning and another turning it back on at the end. The lullaby is our last activity before the goodbye song.

Twinkle, Twinkle, Little Star

Jane Taylor

Traditional

Twin - kle, twin - kle, lit - tle star, how I won - der what you are,
When the blaz - ing sun is gone, when he noth - ing shines up - on,
Then the travel - ler in the dark thanks you for your ti - ny spark, he

up a - bove the world so high, like a dia - mond in the sky,
then you shine your lit - tle light, twin - kle, twin - kle, all the night.
could not see which way to go if you did not twin - kle so,

Twin - kle, twin - kle, lit - tle star, how I won - der what you are.
Twin - kle, twin - kle, lit - tle star, how I won - der what you are.
Twin - kle, twin - kle lit - tle star, how I won - der what you are.

In addition to a cameo appearance by my daughter Ella on the CD (age two at the time of the recording) I've included some of the lesser known verses of "Twinkle, Twinkle". Traditionally a lullaby, I give it the same treatment as the Basque Lullaby (see previous page). Naturally, we only do one lullaby per class so I would do this and the Basque Lullaby in separate programs.

First published in 1806, what strikes me about the lyrics is the historical context: "The traveller in the dark … could not see which way to go, if you did not twinkle so", and "How I wonder what you are". I like to imagine a time when people depended on starlight to see by at night, and when we did not know that the stars we see in the sky are actually suns in other solar systems. How the world has changed, and how I would like to take my daughter to visit a world where the night sky is dark and silent and the only lights are the stars twinkling above us.

Sweet dreams.

Made in the USA
Middletown, DE
04 July 2017